Making A List
and Checking it Twice
Holiday Planner
for Kids

©2021 by Bookfly Publishing, Harvey, Louisiana
Printed in U.S.A
No part of this publication may be reproduced, stored in a retrieval system, or transmitted, in any form or by any means, electronic, mechanical, photocopying, recording, scanning, or otherwise, without the written permission of the publisher. All request or inquiries should be sent to info@bookflypublishing.com
ISBN: 978-1-7369393-3-8
Cover Designer: Nadia Ilchuk
For general information on our products please visit www.bookflypublishing.com. Bookfly Publishing publishes its books in a variety of electronic and print formats. Some content that appears in print may not be available in digital format and vice versa.

Let's get started! It is time to start planning for what some would say the most wonderful time of the year! Even if you been NAUGHTY or NICE it is time to start making a list and checking it twice!

Plan out your month
Do a holiday challenge
Tell a holiday joke
Complete wish list
Write a letter to Santa
Complete gift list
Complete shopping list
Complete to-do list
Read a book
Monitor weekly countdown
Complete an activity page
Get ready for Santa!

Holiday CHRISTMAS Challenges

- Make a Paper Snowflake
- Write a Letter to Santa
- Make a Gingerbread House
- Try a Holiday Dessert
- Read a Holiday Book
- Watch a Holiday Movie
- Create a Holiday Card
- Listen to Holiday Music
- Spread Holiday Cheer

JOKES

What kind of candy does Santa like to eat?

Answer: Jolly Ranchers!

Why did the apple and the Christmas tree cross the road?

Answer: To get to the pineapple!

What did the gingerbread man put on his bed?

Answer: Cookie sheets!

What does an elf learn?

Answer: The elf-a-bet!

What kind of music do elves like to listen to?

Answer: Wrap music!

Why is Santa good at karate?

Answer: Because he has a black belt!

November

Mon	Tue	Wed	Thu	Fri	Sat	Sun

Notes :

December

Mon	Tue	Wed	Thu	Fri	Sat	Sun

Notes :

Mon	Tue	Wed	Thu	Fri	Sat	Sun

Notes :

new year

To Do List

- [ ] --
- [ ] --
- [ ] --
- [ ] --
- [ ] --
- [ ] --
- [ ] --

Weekly Countdown

Date: _____

mon	tue	wed
thu	fri	sat

sun

Mood this Week

notes

Weekly Countdown

Date: _____

mon	tue	wed

thu	fri	sat

sun

Mood this Week

notes

Weekly Countdown

Date: _____

mon	tue	wed
thu	fri	sat
sun		

Mood this Week

notes

Weekly Countdown

Date: _____

mon

tue

wed

thu

fri

sat

sun

Mood this Week

notes

Notes

DOODLE BOARD

shopping list :

Date   On Sale

NO.	GIFT	Y / N

PICTURE BOARD

Holiday Book Review

TITLE	AUTHOR	RATING
		☆☆☆☆☆
		☆☆☆☆☆
		☆☆☆☆☆
		☆☆☆☆☆
		☆☆☆☆☆
		☆☆☆☆☆
		☆☆☆☆☆
		☆☆☆☆☆
		☆☆☆☆☆
		☆☆☆☆☆
		☆☆☆☆☆
		☆☆☆☆☆
		☆☆☆☆☆

Tis the Season	Joy to the World	Happy Holidays
Let it Snow	Peace Love Joy	Merry & Bright
Season's Greetings	Good Tidings	All is Bright

Wishlist

- _____
- _____
- _____
- _____
- _____
- _____
- _____
- _____
- _____
- _____
- _____
- _____
- _____

- _____
- _____
- _____
- _____
- _____
- _____
- _____
- _____
- _____

Holiday Reindeer FOOD *Recipe*

Step 1 ☐ Get A Small Ziploc Bag

Step 2 ☐ Add Oats

Step 3 ☐ Add Green Sprinkles

Step 4 ☐ Add Red Sprinkles

Step 5 ☐ Add White Sprinkles

Step 6 ☐ Add Mini Marshmellows (optional)

Step 7 ☐ Zip/Seal Bag

Step 8 ☐ Shake

Step 9 ☐ Reindeer Ready!

JOURNAL BOARD

Santa Is Coming To Town

Lovely Weather for a Sleigh Ride

O' Christmas Tree

The Season to be Jolly

Sweet Gingerbread

Holly Jolly Christmas

Jingle Jingle All the Way

Santa Letter Templates

Dear Santa,

My name is _____,
I am _____ years old.
This year I would like the following items:

_____

_____

_____

_____

_____

_____

_____

DEAR SANTA,

MY NAME IS _____ .

I AM _____ YEARS OLD.

THIS YEAR I HAVE BEEN:
☐ *Naughty*   ☐ *Nice*

FOR CHRISTMAS, I WOULD LIKE:

_____

_____

_____

_____

_____

Dear Santa,

This year I have been:

- ☐ Nice all year
- ☐ Nice some of the time
- ☐ NAUGHTY (BUT I CAN EXPLAIN!)

My Christmas Wishlist:

_____

_____

_____

_____

_____

_____

                                                  _____

Merry Christmas

www.ingramcontent.com/pod-product-compliance
Lightning Source LLC
Chambersburg PA
CBHW050747110526
44590CB00003B/99